A

DISCOURSE

UPON THE

DUTIES OF A PHYSICIAN,

WITH SOME SENTIMENTS,

ON THE

USEFULNESS AND NECESSITY

OF A

PUBLIC HOSPITAL:

DELIVERED BEFORE THE

PRESIDENT AND GOVERNORS

OF

KING's COLLEGE,

AT THE COMMENCEMENT,

Held on the 16th of MAY, 1769.

As Advice to those GENTLEMEN who then
received the First MEDICAL DEGREES
conferred by that UNIVERSITY.

By SAMUEL BARD, M.D.
Professor of the Practice of Medicine in KING'S COLLEGE.

APPLEWOOD BOOKS
CARLISLE, MASSACHUSETTS

A Discourse upon the Duties of a Physician was first published by A. & J. Robertson of New York in 1769.

Thank you for purchasing an Applewood Book. Applewood reprints America's lively classics— books from the past that are still of interest to modern readers. For a free copy of our current catalog, write to: Applewood Books, 1 River Road, Carlisle, MA 01741.

ISBN 978-1-55709-446-9

Printed and bound in the USA.

10 9 8 7 6 5 4 3 2

Library of Congress Cataloging-in-Publication Data
Bard, Samuel, 1742–1821.
   A discourse upon the duties of a physician / by Samuel Bard.
            p.   cm.
   "First published by A. & J. Robertson of New York in 1769" —T.p. verso.
      ISBN 978-1-55709-446-9
      1 . Medical ethics.   2. Physicians—Conduct of life.
I. Title.
R724.B285   1996
174' .2–dc20   96-9412
                                         CIP

SIR HENRY MOORE, Bart.

Captain General, and Governor in Chief, in and over the *Province* of NEW-YORK, and the Territories depending thereon, in *AMERICA*, Chancellor, and Vice-Admiral of the same.

SIR,

THE favourable Sentiments you were pleased to express of the following Discourse, when it was delivered, and the very generous Warmth with which your Excellency entered into the Proposal it contains, of founding a Public Infirmary in this City, have emboldened the Author to submit it to the Consideration of the Public; and to insure it a favourable Reception, he has ventured to prefix to it your Excellency's Name; not doubting but that the same Benevolence which prompted you so generously to undertake the Cause of the Poor and Unhappy, will now plead his Excuse, for the Liberty he has taken of proposing your Excellency's humane and benevolent Example, to the Imitation of his Fellow Citizens and Country Men.

May your Excellency, and every generous Contributor to this Institution, enjoy the Happiness of seeing the good Effects of your charitable Endeavours; and as the just Reward of your Humanity, may *"the Blessing of him that is ready to perish come upon you."*

In which Hope,
I have the Honor to be,
With the greatest Respect,
Your Excellency's
Most obedient
Humble Servant,
SAMUEL BARD.

THE
PREFACE.

THE Scheme of a Public Hospital for the Reception of the poor Sick of this Government and City, is a Subject, which for a long Time past, has employed the Attention of many charitable and benevolent Inhabitants; particularly of those Gentlemen engaged in the practice of Physic, and Offices of Religion, whose Professions afford them the most frequent Opportunities of knowing the great Necessity there is for such an Institution.

In particular, a Plan has often been proposed, and the most proper Method for putting it in Execution considered, by a Set of Medical Gentlemen, who have formed themselves into a Society for promoting the Knowledge, and extending the Usefulness of their Profession: and it has been a Resolution entered upon the Minutes of that Society, from its first Institution, that they should Address the Legislature upon that Subject, on the first favourable Opportunity.

It likewise has repeatedly been mentioned by the different Professors of Medicine, (particularly Doctors Middleton, and Jones,) in their public

Lectures, and earnestly recommended to the Consideration of the Inhabitants; the unhappy Disputes however, in which we have lately been engaged with our Mother Country, have hitherto rendered their Endeavours fruitless; but, they nevertheless (convinced of the great Necessity there was for such an Institution, and the very great Advantages which all Orders of People must derive from it) resolved to persist in their Endeavours, until some happy Occasion should offer of pushing it with some Probability of Success. Such an Occasion now presents itself, and the Warmth and Zeal, which his Excellency the Governor, and most of his honorable Council, have expressed for it, and the Liberality, with which they have subscribed towards it, induce them to think the present, the fittest Time, for recommending it, to the serious Consideration of the Public.

And as an Institution of this Nature, must necessarily be calculated for the Benefit of the distressed of all Sects and Persuasions whatsoever, it is hoped, that the generous and public spirited of every Denomination, will enter warmly into the Design, and promote it with that Zeal, which should actuate the Breast of every Man, who thinks it his Duty to relieve the Necessities of his Fellow Creatures, or promote the Happiness of Society.

A

DISCOURSE

UPON THE

DUTIES OF A PHYSICIAN

Homines ad Deos, nulla re proprius accedunt, quam Salutem Hominibus dando. CICERO.

There is nothing by which a Man approaches nearer to the Perfections of the Deity, than by restoring the Sick, to the Enjoyment of the Blessings of Health.

THAT this Country has, ever since its Discovery and Settlement, laboured under the greatest Disadvantages, from the imperfect Manner, in which Students have been instructed in the Principles of Medicine; and from the Consequent prevailing Ignorance of but too many of its Professors; is a Truth which cannot be contested; and of which many unhappy Families have severely felt the fatal Effects.

The present Occasion therefore must give the most real Pleasure to every considerate Man, or Lover of his Country; and surely there is no Friend of Learning, but must rejoice to see these Gentlemen, who have given the most public and ample Testimony of their Abilities, now soliciting the Honors of this University, in a Profession hitherto (at least in a regular Manner) uncultivated amongst us.

I am therefore particularly happy in having this Opportunity of congratulating every public spirited Friend and Patron of this College, and especially those of the medical Institution, upon the present Instance of its Success, which affords so pleasing a Prospect of its rising Reputation and future Utility.

But it is to you, Gentlemen, who are Candidates for medical Degrees, that I mean in a more particular Manner to address my present Discourse; receive then my Thanks for the Honors you have already reflected upon us, and as both for your Sakes and our own, I cannot but be anxious for your future

Reputation; let me once more, before we part, request your Attention for a few Moments, whilst I endeavour to explain to you the weighty duties of your Profession—A Profession, in the Practice of which, Integrity and Abilities, will place you among the most useful; and Ignorance and Dishonesty, among the most pernicious Members of Society.

And be not alarmed, if I set out with telling you, that your Labours must have no End. No less than Life, and its greatest Blessing Health, are to be the Objects of your Attention; and would you acquit yourselves to your own Consciences, you must spend *your* Days in assiduous Enquiries, after the Means of rendering those of others long and happy.

Do not therefore imagine, that from this Time your Studies are to cease; so far from it, you are to be considered as but just entering upon them; and unless your whole Lives, are one continued Series of Application and Improvement, you will fall short of your Duty. For, if in the Eye of the Law, the Man who does not afford, to all immediately under his Care and Protection, as far as in him lies, the necessary Means of preserving Life, is considered as accessary to Murder, how will that Physician excuse himself to his own Conscience, or what Palliation of his Guilt, will he plead at the awful Bar of eternal Justice, who instead of embracing and industriously cultivating every Opportunity of Improvement, shall (conscious of his own Inability) rashly tamper with the Lives of his Fellow Creatures; and, at the risk of their Safety, defraud them of their Property? Would not any one consider the Lawyer an Impostor, not to use a harsher Phrase, who, conscious of his own Ignorance, should give Advice, which might endanger the Estate of another? And is not the Physician who imposes Ignorance upon me for Knowledge, and puts my Life to the hazard of an uncertain die; so much the greater Impostor, in as much as my Life, is of greater Estimation than my Estate. In a Profession then, like that you have embraced, where the Object is of so great Importance as the Life of a Man; you are accountable even for the Errors of Ignorance, unless you have embraced every Opportunity of obtaining Knowledge.

And to a Man, who has any Conscience at all, it will be but a slight Alleviation of his Remorse, to say, after some fatal Blunder, *I knew no better!* Unless he can likewise add, that it is to be attributed to the Frailty of his Nature, and not to the Negligence of his Disposition, that he was not better informed. Nor will a weeping Parent receive much Consolation from this Reflection, that by the fatal Ignorance of his Physician, and not by the malignancy of the Disease, he has been robbed of the Staff and Support of his Life, the Joy and Comfort of his declining Age.

Did I know a Wretch among the Practitioners of Medicine, whose insensible Soul neither feels for the Distresses he may Occasion, nor partakes in the Joys he may give rise to; I say, did I know a Man so void of every Sentiment of Tenderness, and Humanity; I would advise him, from Motives of Interest and Gain, to endeavour at the Attainment of Skill in his Profession. But to you, Gentlemen, I will point out the Gratification inseparable from the Acquisition of Knowledge, that ever to be wished for Praise, which falls from the Lips of the Wise and the Virtuous, and Applause of an approving Conscience, and the unspeakable Pleasure of doing good, as the Reward of all your Toil, and as the strongest Spur to your future Industry.

As to those who have neither Emulation nor Honesty, who neither have Abilities, nor will give themselves the Trouble of acquiring them; I would recommend it to such, seriously to consider the Sixth Commandment,

'THOU SHALT DO NO MURDER.'

In the Prosecution of your Studies, let such Authors as have transmitted to us Observations founded upon Nature, claim your particular Attention. Of these, HIPPOCRATES shines the foremost; his unwearied Diligence in observing and collecting the Symptoms of Diseases, his Fidelity and

Accuracy in relating them, his happy Facility in discovering their Causes, his almost prophetic Knowledge of their Events, and his successful Treatment of them, can never be sufficiently admired, and will hand down his Name, with Honor and Applause to the latest Posterity.

A few others among the Ancients, who have followed the Steps of Hippocrates, are well worth your Perusal; but whilst you acknowledge *their* Merit, do not affect the Pedantry of despising the Moderns; and carefully avoid that Rock, upon which most of the fond Admirers of Antiquity have split, a blind and slavish Attachment to its Opinions; the Bar where Truth has been so often Shipwrecked, and which more than the want of Ingenuity or Capacity, stopped the Progress of Learning for above twelve hundred Years.

Why should we give more to those Times, than they attributed to themselves? Read the Writings of the wisest among the Ancients, and they are filled with Modesty and Diffidence, why then should we ascribe to them, Infallibility and Omniscience? They doubted the Assertions, and controverted the Opinions of the Times which preceded them; why should not we doubt and controvert theirs; and leave to Posterity the Liberty of controverting ours? Let us then examine their Writings with Candour, but with Freedom, and embrace or reject their Opinions; as they shall be found consistent, or inconsistent with later Experience.

Without therefore depreciating the Merit of the Ancients, let us do Justice to their Posterity, and do not from an over Zeal for Antiquity, sacrifice Sydenham and Boerhaave, to the Manes of Hippocrates and Galen.—I see no Reason why Time only should lessen our Abilities, and surely Experience must increase our Knowledge: and although I think some of the Ancients may be read with great Advantage; yet it is the most celebrated Moderns (who with equal Abilities enjoy the additional Advantage of near 2000 Years of Experience) whom I would recommend to your most attentive

Perusal; particularly those great Ornaments of their Profession, SYDENHAM, BOERHAAVE, HUXHAM, PRINGLE, and WHYTT; and some others of our latest English and Scotch Physicians, *"Horum Scripta nocturna versate manu, versate diurna."*

In your Intercourse with your Fellow Practitioners, let Integrity, Candour, and Delicacy be your Guides. There is a particular Sensibility of Disposition, which seems essential to delicate Honor, and which I believe is the best Counterpoise to Self-Interest. This I would by all Means advise you to cultivate, as you will meet with many Occasions where it only can direct your Conduct.

Never affect to despise a Man for the want of a regular Education, and treat even harmless Ignorance, with Delicacy and Compassion, but when you meet with it joined with foolhardiness and Presumption, you must give it no quarter.

On no Pretence whatever, practice those little Arts of Cunning and Dissimulation, which to the Scandal of the Profession, have been but too frequent among us. Nor ever attempt to raise your Fame on the Ruins of another's Reputation; and remember that you ought not only to be cautious of your Words, a Shrug or a Whisper, the stare of Surprise, or a piteous Exclamation of Sorrow, more effectually wound another's Reputation, and more clearly betray the Baseness of a Man's own Heart, than the loudest Expressions.

Do not pretend to Secrets, Panacea's, and Nostrums, they are illiberal, dishonest, and inconsistent with your Characters, as Gentlemen and Physicians, and with your Duty as Men—For if you are possessed of any valuable Remedy, it is undoubtedly your Duty to divulge it, that as many as possible may reap the Benefit of it; and if not, (which is generally the Case) you are propagating a Falsehood, and imposing upon Mankind.

In your Behaviour to the Sick, remember always that your Patient is the Object of the tenderest Affection, to some one, or perhaps to many about him; it is therefore your Duty, not only to endeavour to preserve his Life, but to avoid wounding the Sensibility of a tender Parent, a distressed Wife, or an affectionate Child. Let your Carriage be humane and attentive, be interested in his Welfare, and shew your Apprehension of his Danger, rather by your Assiduity to relieve, than by any harsh or brutal Expressions of it. On the other hand, never buoy up a dying Man with groundless Expectations of Recovery, this is at best a good natured and humane Deception, but too often it arises from the baser Motives of Lucre and Avarice: besides, it is really cruel, as the stroke of Death is always most severely felt, when unexpected; and the grim Tyrant may in general be disarmed of his Terrors, and rendered familiar to the most timid, and apprehensive; either by frequent Meditation, by the Arguments of Philosophy, or by the Hopes and Promises of Religion. But even overlooking the important Concerns of Futurity; the Business of this Life may render such a Conduct highly dangerous and criminal; as those to whom the thoughts of Death are painful, are too apt when flattered with the Prospect of

Recovery, to neglect the necessary Provision against a Disappointment, and by that Means involve their Families in Confusion and Distress.

Above all Things, avoid any ridiculous Expressions of Humour, at the bed-side of a sick Man; you cannot chuse a more unseasonable Opportunity for your Mirth; nor will you find a Person of a generous and benevolent Disposition, who can smile at the Repetition of a Witticism, which carries with it the Appearance of so much Inhumanity.

Let your Prescriptions be simple, and as neat and agreeable as the Nature of the Remedy will permit—Nothing can be more absurd than the Farrago of some, nothing more disgustful than the Slovenliness of others; for it is impossible to learn the true Virtues of Medicines, from compound Prescriptions; and Inelegance frequently disappoints us of their Effects. — And as it is probable, from the Mode of Practice in this Country, that you will not only be the Prescribers, but likewise the Dispensers of your

Medicines, let your Integrity be proof against the Temptation of unnecessarily multiplying Prescriptions, and trust rather to the Liberality of your Patient, than to the Quantity of your Physic, for your Reward. For altho' perhaps by this Method you may sometimes think your Services undervalued, yet you will always enjoy the superior Satisfaction of conscious Rectitude, which, by an honest Man, will ever be preferred to a trifling Emolument.—

In the Infancy of this Country, the present Mode of practising Medicine was necessarily introduced, from the Scarcity, both of Inhabitants and Physicians. But in so populous a City as this, it is beyond a Doubt, that the Regulations it is now under, are both injurious to the Inhabitants, and dishonorable to the Profession: yet I confess it is not very easy to point out a Remedy to the Inconveniences attendant on it. There is but one, and that perhaps at present would not be thought expedient; but until it is, those who are in good Circumstances must rely wholly upon the Integrity of their

Physicians; and for the Poor who are the greatest sufferers, we must endeavour to find out some other Source of Relief.

Whenever you shall be so unhappy as to fail, in your Endeavours to relieve; let it be your constant Aim to convert, particular Misfortunes into general Blessings, by carefully inspecting the Bodies of the Dead, inquiring into the Causes of their Diseases, and thence improving your own Knowledge, and making further and useful Discoveries in the healing Art.

Nor can I help regretting the many Obstacles you will meet with in prosecuting this so necessary an Enquiry; from the Prejudices of the People in general, and a false Tenderness and mistaken Delicacy in Relations. Time and Perseverance however must overcome popular Prejudices, and will I hope before long, remove these Difficulties, and open this Door to Medical Improvement.

Let those who are at once the unhappy Victims, both of Poverty and Disease, claim your particular Attention; I cannot represent to myself a more real Object of Charity, than a poor Man with perhaps a helpless Family, labouring under the complicated Miseries of Sickness and Penury. Paint to yourselves the agonizing feelings of a Parent, whilst labouring under some painful Disease, he beholds a helpless Offspring around his Bed, in want of the necessaries of Nature; imagine the Despair of an affectionate Wife, and a tender Mother, who can neither relieve the Pain and Anxiety of her Husband, nor supply the importunate cravings of her Children; and *then* deny them your Assistance if you can— but the Supposition is injurious to Humanity, and *you* in particular, I know want no such Incitements to Duty and Benevolence. I cannot however help regretting, the very frequent Opportunities you will meet with, particularly in this Place, of exercising your Humanity upon such Occasions; owing to the want of a proper Asylum, for such unhappy and real Objects of Charity it is truly a reproach, that a City like this, should want a public Hospital, one of the most useful and necessary charitable Institutions that can possibly be imagined.

The labouring Poor are allowed to be the support of the Community; their Industry enables the Rich to live in Ease and Affluence, and it is from the Hands of the Manufacturer we derive, not only the Necessaries, but the Superfluities of Life; whilst the poor Pittance he earns will barely supply the Necessities of Nature, and it is literally by the sweat of his Brow, that he gains his daily Subsistance; how heavy a Calamity must Sickness be to such a Man, which putting it out of his Power to work, immediately deprives him and perhaps a helpless Family of Bread!

Nor would the good Effects of an Hospital be wholly confined to the Poor, they would extend to every Rank, and greatly contribute to the Safety and Welfare of the whole Community. Every Country has its particular Diseases; the Varieties of Climate, Exposure, Soil, Situation, Trades, Arts, Manufactures, and even the Character of a People, all pave the Way to new Complaints, and vary the Appearance of those, with which we are already acquainted; Hence Ægypt is subject to the Plague; Holland to Intermittents; the West-Indies to Putrid; and the Northern Countries to inflammatory Diseases; and Spain and England to Hypochondriacal Complaints; which reigning Diseases of a Country, not only have Peculiarities of their own, but often vary the Characters of such as are common to that Country with others, and these Peculiarities with their Antidotes can properly be learned only in public Hospitals, where having a number of Sick at one Time, not only affords and Opportunity of the better comparing and remarking their Symptoms, but they being under a certain Discipline and Regulation, the Faces of their diseases are not changed, either by the indulgence of friends or the officiousness of Nurses; which is too often the case in private practice. Another argument, (and that by no means the least,) for an Institution of this Nature, is, that it affords the best and only means of properly instructing Pupils in the Practice of Medicine; as far therefore, as the breeding good and able Physicians, which in all Countries and at all Times has been thought an object of the highest Importance, deserves the Consideration of the Public, this Institution must likewise claim its Protection and Encouragement.

Nor is the Scheme of a Public Hospital I believe so impracticable, nor the Execution of it, I hope at so great a distance, as at first sight it may appear to be. There are Numbers in this Place I am sure (was a Subscription once set on foot, upon an extensive and generous Plan) whose Fortunes enable them, and whose Benevolence would prompt them, liberally to contribute to so useful an Institution; it wants but a Prime Mover, whose Authority would give Weight to the Undertaking, and whose Zeal and Industry, would promote it. Such a one I hope ere long to see rise up amongst us, and may the Blessing of the Poor, and the Applause of the Good and Humane, be the Reward of his Assiduity and Labour.

FINIS.

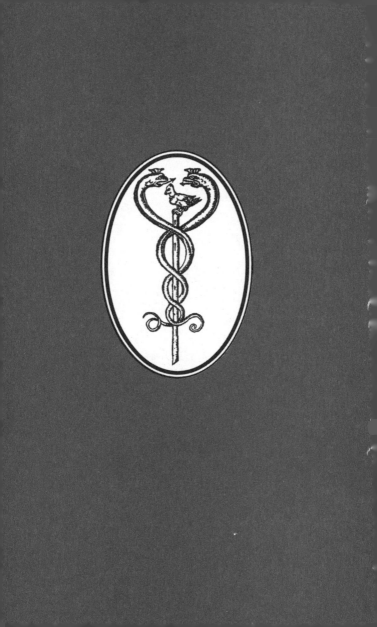